The Berlin Dictionary

Edited and Illustrated by
Rachelle Beaudoin

Enjoy!,

Rachelle Beaudoin

Published by Boom Pier Press, 395 Old Street Road Peterborough NH, 03458,USA.

berlindictionary@gmail.com

The greatest care has been taken in compiling this book. However, no responsibility can be accepted by the publishers, sponsors or compilers for the accuracy of the information presented.

Printed in the United States.

ISBN 978-0-557-19739-2

To my husband Steve my partner in life
and on this project

Introduction

This project started as a conversation between my husband Steve, also a Berlin native, and I on a drive home to Berlin for the Easter holiday. I had completed one art project about Berlin and still felt compelled to create more. As we discussed the places we wanted to visit on our trip, The East Side Mall, Mary's, the Pub, we realized that these places might seem foreign to non-natives. There were other times when speaking to each other when I would have to stop and ask if what I had just said was a "real" word or a "Berlin" word. Does anyone else know what a mousse is? Why do people stare at me strangely when I say "piton?"

And so the Berlin Dictionary was born.

I was also drawn to this project because of the changes and challenges that the city and its citizens having been facing over the past few years. There has been a lot of discussion about Berlin's future and about its changing identity. The dictionary seemed like a way to get people to take pride in or poke fun at aspects of the community while recognizing and enjoying its uniqueness. I hoped that this list of terms could help define the city in some small way. I felt it could help us see what needs to be let go, what is best left in the past and what is worth maintaining.

Language is fluid, living and adaptable. We see this in the hybrid words, invented phrases and nicknames collected in this dictionary. I am hopeful that the city will change, adapt and grow just as the language used by its residents always has.

I set out to create a participatory dictionary with the words coming from residents, former residents and neighbors. It was not long after I put out news of the project that I began receiving responses. The submissions came from Berlin and beyond. Each day I was delighted to find new words had come in. I am sure you will see there is a range of words coming from a range of time periods, age groups and experiences. It is not accurate to list me as the author since there were over 70 co-authors to this book. My work involved collecting and organizing of the information and, of course, drawing the pictures.

Although there were many contributors, this list is far from exhaustive. If you think of a word we have omitted please send it along via the information given at the back of the book. There are many variations of words and the way you use or spell a word might be different from the way the contributor submitted it. I must also note that the spelling of the words, especially those rooted in Canadian French and coming out of the Franco-American tradition, has been difficult to say the least. I have included multiple spellings of some popular words. It was not uncommon to have a single word submitted with five different spellings. Many contributors noted that they were unsure of the spelling but they sent along their best guess. Many of the words submitted and used in Berlin are standard French or slight variations on standard French. Several of the French words are not unique to Berlin but are used in some form in other New England Franco-American communities.

I would like to thank Steven Roberge for helping with the conception and completion of the project; my mother, Debbie Beaudoin for supporting me in the research and editing; the Roberge's for their creative words and enthusiasm for the project; Robert Perreault of Saint Anselm College for his expertise, interest and point of view on the project; Don Fournier for his knowledge of Berlin-French; Shawn Marquis and Rich Goyette for their creative efforts surrounding LogJam; Sarah Wetherbee for reading the manuscript, my grandparents and my father, the late Renaud Beaudoin since they are the reason I am from Berlin in the first place and finally, the contributors since without them, there would be no book.

The contributors are listed in alphabetical order each with a number and a list of words they submitted. In the dictionary, you will see numbers next to submitted words corresponding to the person who submitted said word.

This project was inspired by the *New American Dictionary* by the Institute for Infinitely Small Things and by community-based art projects by John Ewing, Christopher Robbins and Carmen Montoya.

Rachelle Beaudoin
2009

1st-7th Holes[1] (Noun) The swimming holes along the Peabody river. The temperature of the water is usually in the 50-55 degree range.
Let's go swimming at Third Hole.

7 (Seven, the)[60] (Noun) The snow pack in King's Ravine forms the shape of a seven that is used to deduce the passing seasons.
The 7 is still there so it's not summer yet.

7th Street Graphics (Noun) A print and design shop located on Glen Avenue.
I am going to 7th Street Graphics on Glen Ave to pick up my sweet truck decals.

13 Mile Woods [23, 33] (Noun) The 18 mile stretch of Route 16 between Milan and Errol, plagued with moose, frost heaves, and leaf peepers. Named so because of the woods that line the road leading from Milan to Errol.
Did you drive through 13 Mile Woods? The roads are terrible!

8084 eight-oh-eight-four (Noun) A band that thrived in Berlin in the 80s and early 90s.
Man, did you hear 8084 last night at the Sanborn (see Sanborn) they brought the house down.

a guog dons[45] (Interjection) An interjection of pain.
A guog dons that hurt!

absolutely[66] (Adverb) A monosyllable expression uttered as answer to any number of varied questions.
Is the sky blue? Absolutely.

Alcohol Springs [23] (Noun) A large sandpit in Success well known as a place to target practice, light fireworks, and burn tires.
I'm going shooting at Alcohol Springs.

aller à fall, on va en fall[7, 54, 27, 13, 10 , 45] (Verb) To go downtown (going to the falls) This expression was used by East Side residents as they referred to going down town. This expression was used for many years even after the name of the city had been changed from Berlin Falls to Berlin. The falls refers to the area of Main Street where a dam on the Androscoggin River created a waterfall.
Je vais aller en fall.

Andy, the AKA The Androscoggin River, The River, (Noun) The Androscoggin River flows from Errol to Brunswick before empting into the Atlantic Ocean. The river is central to the identity of Berlin NH as it geographically divides the city and was used historically to push logs into the local paper mills.
Fernald took his canoe out on the Andy for a leisurely paddle.

an-téka, en tout cas[18] en toués cas (French) Anyways or in any case.

Arena, the[33] (Noun) most beloved, used and well appreciated recreation building built by Fr. Bousquet, home base for the high school hockey teams and for the great Berlin Maroons Hockey team, and in the summer it was roller skating rink. See also Norte Dame Arena.
Let's go to the game down at the Arena.

arguine [49] (Noun) saw.

arnt (Noun) Aunt
My Arnt Jeannette took me out shopping downtown for the afternoon.

arrête de baver[49] (Verb) to talk for nothing. Literally stop dribbling.

arrête de limoner[49] (Verb) stop fussing.

arrête de shinger[49] (Verb) stop complaining.

arrêtte de babiner[49] (Verb) stop talking for nothing.

l'assiette[72] (Noun) Dinner plate.

at camp (Noun) Going up to Camp- (Verb) A rudimentary second home, lake house, river house, that is used primarily for recreation and is not up to date and may or may not have functional plumbing. The phrase At Camp, refers to the place itself. Going to Camp refers to the action of going and staying there.

Who's at camp? The whole family is heading up to camp for the weekend.

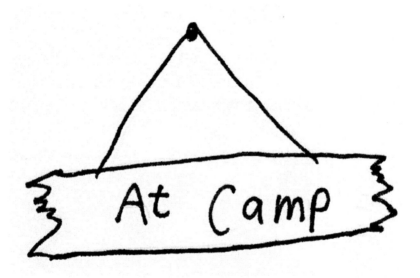

au bain, eh bien [44] (Interjection) Oh well.

Avenues, the[50] (Noun) 1-6th Avenue section of Berlin.
Did you ride up to Tammy's house in the Avenues?

banking[19,63] (bankin') (Noun) A hill or "embankment" in the rest of the English-speaking world. Also bank of snow, sand or wall.
I can't see over the banking.

barbotte also babout,[23,15,33,9] (Noun) Horned pout, catfish, bullhead.
It's a warm night, want to go barbotte fishing?

bark field[1] (Noun) Excess bark that was used to fill vacant lots, etc. There was a field on the East side that was used when all the other fields were covered with snow.
Go take some bark from the bark field for mulch.

baroutette[49] (Noun) Wheelbarrow.

Batouille or Bataille[33] (Noun) A card game, in English called War.

Beat the Bonhomme[23] (Noun) Another name for the card game Solitaire. See also bonhomme.
I'm bored so I will play Beat the Bonhomme.

bécosse or becuss[49] [16] (Noun) Backhouse, outhouse or bathroom also meaning to go use the bathroom.

beeno[52] (Noun) Bingo. See also bino.
She is always lucky at beeno.

Ben coudon!, Bien écoute donc![18] (Interjection) What the heck!

ben wéyons don, bien voyons donc![18] I don't believe it. Well let's see.

Berlin[6] (Noun) (BUR-lin) The largest city in Northern New Hampshire along the banks of the Androscoggin River that was formerly the center of the pulp and paper industry of New England.
I am from Berlin, no, not Germany. There's one in New Hampshire.

Berliny (Adjective) The state of being from Berlin or of Berlin. To have Berlin qualities.
I just met Tina last night. She's pretty Berliny.

Berlin Brown Trout[25] (Noun) Slang for floating garbage and/or sewage in the Androscoggin and Dead rivers; usually associated with industrial facilities.
The only things that fishermen could catch below the mill were Berlin Brown Trout.

Berlin City Bank Rotating Cube Sign (Noun) A large electric rotating cube sign that sat at the corner of Pleasant St and Green St. It advertised the Berlin City Bank, had a clock and thermometer. When properly functioning the cube slowly rotated but it was often stuck and remained on one side.

The Berlin City Bank sign said it was 78 degrees today. It must be in the sun.

Berlin Daily Sun (Noun) AKA The Free Paper, Daily Sun- a local free daily or almost daily newspaper whose highlights include sports, Once Upon A Berlin Time and the police log. *They were all out of the Free Paper at TeaBirds.* *Did you see the article about the City Council in the Daily Sun?*

Berlin Dairy Bar (Noun) See also DB or Northland Dairy Bar.

Berlin 'do, the (Noun) A hairstyle for women popular in Berlin for much longer than in the rest of the United States (see Granite Curtain) that involves short layers in front and spiky and short back section. This could also refer to an updo of similar styling that replaces the short spikey section with curls.
Jill just got a new haircut, it is the basic Berlin 'Do.

Berlin Heights[50] (Noun) Prospect St., Church St. area of Berlin.
My cousins lived in Berlin Heights.

Berlin Heights Addition[50] (Noun) Obscure; area of Berlin further up Madison Ave., Willard St., top of Park St.

Berlin High School (Noun) The local public High School located on Willard St. whose mascot is the Mountaineer. See also Patio. See also DL.
I went up to the high school for the Open House.

Berlin Junior High (Noun) The public Junior High School on located on State Street. Home of the Mounties'.
Stephanie remembered her time at Berlin Junior High School as incredibly awkward but still fun.

Berlin Junior High Auditorium (Noun) A large gathering space for plays, events and ceremonies located at the Junior High.
I went to the high school musical at the Auditorium.

Berlin Mafia (Noun) The men at St. Anne Church who wear suits with lapel pins and take your money during the collection.

Berlin Maroons (Noun) Old Time Hockey.
The Berlin Maroons produced some fantastic hockey players.

Berlin Mills[33] (Noun) A section of Berlin running along the river and the paper mill, on upper Main Street.

Berlin Motor Inn (Noun) A motel in the center of Berlin.
There is no room at the Berlin Motor Inn.

Berlin Reporter AKA The Berlin Repeater (Noun) A local newspaper that was once daily that reports on events, sports and community news.
Please pass me the sports section of the Reporter.

Bernie and Dave's [21] [60] (Noun) a restaurant that was located on Glen Ave. in Berlin.
Do you remember going out to eat at Bernie and Dave's?

Betty Dee's (Noun) a formal dress and bridal shop located on Main St.
After I go tanning, I need to pick up my prom dress from Betty Dee's.

BG Road (Noun) The Berlin-Gorham Road.   Route 16.
Dan got an enormous ticket for speeding on the BG Road.

bi-bit, bibite, bibit [28] [23] [17] [63] (Noun) A small bug, any type of small bug. Variation: Fashion Bi-bit meaning Fashion Bug.
Did you bring some bug spray to keep the bibbits away?

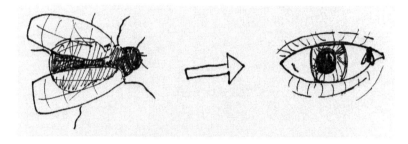

Big Bella[14] (Noun) A bell that is rung for search and rescue missions.
We need to get Big Bella out for search and rescue during hunting season.

big, big, big (Adjective) When something is really big.
We've got a dead tree in our yard and it's big big big.

big hand (Noun) A large fiberglass hand advertising fiberglass art on Glen Ave in Berlin.
You drive past the IGA and then turn right at the Big Hand.

bino[70] (Noun) Bingo.
I won twenty dollars at the VFW Bino.

Bisson's Sugar House (Noun) A Maple Sugar house located on Cates Hill in Berlin.
She craved Maple Taffy from Bisson's Sugar House.

la bizoot [20] (Noun) The joker in the card game Pitch.

black bears (Noun) Bears that are black. Common visitors.
I saw a black bear and three cubs on High Street last night.

Blanchette's Sausage[23] (Noun) A sausage invented by the Blanchette family of Berlin loved for its secret combination of spices.
I'm hungry for some Blanchette's Sausage.

bleeding Jesus (Noun) A crucifix located in St. Joseph's church that appeared to bleeding, causing long lines of onlookers to descend onto the church. As seen in *Weird New England* by Joseph A. Citro.
After lab testing, turns out the bleeding Jesus was fake.

blessing the field (Verb) A secret ritual performed by the Berlin High School field hockey team before tournament games.
After the spaghetti supper, we went to bless the field.

blizzard of 69 (Noun) A severe snow storm the likes of which had not been seen.
Remember the Blizzard of 69?

bob house (Noun) An ice fishing shack or ice shanty.
I just put my bob house out on Pontook.

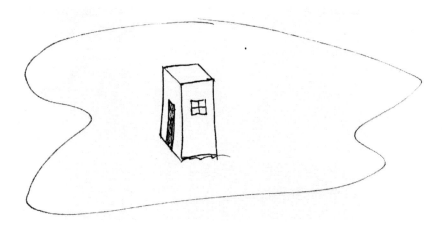

Bob's Store (Noun) One of the remaining corner stores in Berlin, stocked with candy and beer, with a prime location next to the Notre Dame Arena.
You can go down to Bob's Store for all I care! Can you pick up some ice at Bob's?

Bodyline, the (Noun) A gym in Berlin that operates on an honor system, with handmade and other fitness equipment.
Meet me up at the Bodyline to pump some iron.

boiler, the (Noun) The large structure at the Mill with the smokestack used to produce energy for the Mill's operation.
The priest had to speak louder when the boiler released its steam.

bonfire (Noun) Also to have a fire. 1. A large fire set during homecoming for students to burn both pieces of their float and effigies of opposing teams. 2. A recreational fire set to stand or sit around.
Jerry's having a bonfire at his house tonight.

bonhomme [12, 23] (Noun) 1. Fisher Price Little People with no arms. 2. A man, especially old or good. Variation: bonhomme de neige meaning snowman. The female equivalent is bonnefemme.

1. The little boy entertained himself by playing with his bonhommes.

2. I saw a bonhomme walking down Main Street.

boom piers (Noun) Small manmade islands on the Androscoggin River that were historically used to secure a chain of boom logs that divided the river in order to sort logs between Brown Paper Company and International Paper Company as they were driven down river to the mills.

Be sure to take a picture of the boom pier. Gaston took his boat out to the boom pier and enjoyed a picnic lunch.

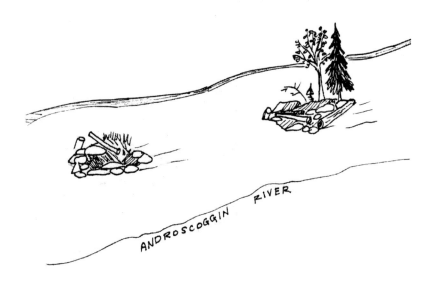

bouder[9] (Verb) To pout. See also boudin.

boudin [9, 38] (Noun) Blood sausage.

bra-attelage[18] (Noun) A bra hung on the clothesline.
My father said he didn't want to see my bra-attelage waving in the wind.

braquette or briquette[49] Tack.

brenleu[65] (Noun) Someone who is extremely slow (e.g., a Sunday driver.)

broom the floor (Verb) Sweep the floor using a broom.
Be sure to broom the floor, there, before your company arrives.

broomball (Noun) A game similar to ice hockey played on ice wearing rubberized shoes. Each team has 5 players plus a goalkeeper on the ice at one time. The object of the game is to score goals by hitting a small ball past a goaltender using sticks resembling small brooms.
We stayed up all night during the 24 hour broomball tournament.

Brown Company Store[33] (Noun) Located in Berlin Mills, a large store run by Brown Company for its employees. It supplied a variety of items including groceries, tools and general inventory. It was accessible by bus line.

Bud Man [23] (Noun) The official mascot of the Ferco recycling plant.
Bring all your cans up to the Bud Man.

bulkhead[19] (Noun) An outside cellar door.

Bulldog Sauce [23] (Noun) An Asian fruit and vegetable sauce used as a condiment at the Yokohama and at home. Technically known as Tonkatsu Sauce. Aslo see IGA. Also see Kushi Kato.
I need some more Bulldog sauce for my kushis.

butin[48] (Noun) Clothes.
Je vais laver mon butin. (I will wash my clothes.)

c'est baveu[49] (Adjective) It's bad weather. Literally, it is slobbering.

c'est bon[20] (Verb) "I pass" in the card game Pitch. Literally, it's good.

ça fait dur[49] (Adjective) It is ugly. Literally it is hard. Also it is hard or difficult to endure.

ça flippe? [46][75] How's it going? Flippe is a corruption of "feel" in the sense of how do you feel today? There's also a French word "filer" meaning "to spin" which sounds like "to feel" and in 12th century French, it was used in the figurative sense to "feel well" and "feel badly." Literally, it referred to knots in thread when spinning, so if there were no knots, then "ça file ben" and if there were knots tangling your thread, then ça file mal."
Comment ça flippe? Ça flippe.

ça pique or pic[20] A phrase used for cheating in cards telling your partner that you have spades.

ça c'est une coureuse[7] [75] (Noun) An expression used to describe "loose" women. A coureuse is a female runner, meaning that she runs from here to there. Variation: coureur de bois, literally runner of the woods which refers to early French and French-Canadian explorers and fur trappers.

ca c'est une gasse[7] or garce (Noun) An expression to describe a "vicious" woman. Garce comes from the word garcon meaning a very masculine girl.

câlice (Noun, Adjective) Literally the chalice in Roman Catholicism. A colorful swear word. Variation: câdis. This is more commonly used in Berlin as a way to avoid cursing the chalice.
Eh câlice! Ehh cadis!

can-a-rabish or canne-a-robbiche[65] (Noun) Garbage can.

Canuck[44] (Noun) French Canadian/Native Indian heritage.

caoutchouc[5] (Noun) Rubber that is worn over shoes. In Franglais, rubbeurs.

capot[46] (Noun) A coat.

caribou[9] (Noun) Wine and whiskey drink.

Cascade Flats (Noun) A neighborhood in Gorham on lower land near the river and near one section of the papermill. See also Mary's Pizza. See also the Flats.
Fred drove through the Cascade Flats on his way home last night.

Cascade Hill[33] (Noun) A neighborhood built on a large hill, which began at Western Avenue and led into Berlin, up on the hill was St. Benedict's Catholic School and Church and Lemerise's grocery store.

Catello's and Sons (Noun) Music shop on Glen Ave in Berlin with a sign that lets you know who's getting married at the Chalet See Chalet. See also 8084 and Level 10.
Dude, check out this new guitar I got from Catello's.

Cates Hill (Noun) Rural hill in Berlin with such landmarks as Bisson's Sugar House and Grand View.
We drove up to Cates Hill to watch the sunset.

ce fais encroire se faire accroire [9][75] (Adjective) Vain. Similar to saying "He thinks he's ..." followed by some pretentious comment about himself.

Cedar Pond (Noun) A pond in Milan NH with homes, camps and a campground.
Let's go ice fishing up at Cedar Pond.

cel or sel[72] (Noun) Salt.

char[65] (Noun) Car.

Chalet, the (Noun) A function hall and music venue in Berlin NH.
There is going to be a benefit concert at the Chalet this weekend.

chien qui passe [43] [75] (sha ki pawse) (Adjective) An idiom meaning disheveled, unkempt. Literally referring to a stray cat or stay dog.

chicka-blaow [41] Onomatopoeia for a bass / wah-wah guitar sound made famous in the soundtracks of pornographic movies created in the 1970's. Outside of Berlin it is pronounced bow chick bow wow.
Kelly and I had dinner at the Toi-Chan, tipped a few back at The Green Parrot, got home and then chicka-blaow!

Chinese pie [21, 61, 38, 39] (Noun) Also known as "Pâté Chinois" (Pa-tay Shin-wa) is commonly called a "Shepherd's Pie" in other parts of the world. The ingredients are: ground beef, cream corn or regular corn, and mashed potatoes (layered in that order from bottom to top) and is baked in the oven. It was listed as "Chinese Pie" on the high school menu when it was served.

Who wants to eat some Chinese pie?

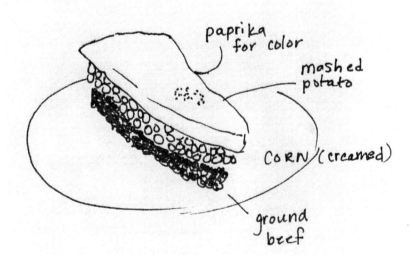

Choo-Choos (Noun) A downtown diner. . .a great place to meet.
Linda and Richard met for lunch at Choo-Choos.

chou[9] (Noun/Adverb) dear.   As in "mon petit chou." Literally it is "my little cabbage."

Christmas Tree Plant (Noun) An industrial plant that manufactures Little Trees car air fresheners located on Rt 110. The trees are world renown and very potent.
Leslie works over at the Christmas Tree Plant.

chtedis, J'te dis [18 75] I tell you. Also let me tell you. "Je" (I) is often pronounced as a "ch" in French, but "ch" in French is pronounced like "sh" in English.

chu tout fourré, Je suis tout [18 75] (Adverb) I am so confused. Alos I am licked or I am defeated in the sense of a game.

chu dans' lune. Je suis dans la lune[18] (Adjective) I am spaced out. Literally in the moon.

City Hall (Noun) The local hub for government, meetings, and permitting. It also contains an auditorium.
We had to go to City Hall to get our fire permit for the bonfire.

close the lights [17] (Verb) See also Open the lights. To turn off the lights.

Club, the [33, 21] (Noun) The alternate name for the YMCA, the famous Community Club run by Bill Roach for years where kids would go to learn to swim, participate in bowling leagues, use pool tables and roller skate. The building was erected for the town by the Brown family. It was located on the East Side by Community Field. Popular during the 40s and 50s.

cochonnerie, chochonerie [44 75] (Noun) Garbage. From the word cochon meaning pig. Cochonnerie can be taken both literally and figuratively

Community Field (Noun) A park, baseball fields, basketball courts and skateboard ramp in the shadow of the Berlin mill.
It was a glorious day at Community field, the air was fresh, the sun was shining and it was 50 degrees and the girls won their softball game.

cookies [61] (Noun) When you spin your car, motorcycle or 4-wheeler around in circles either on dirt, snow, or ice. Referred to as "doing a cookie."

coquottes or cocottes [17] (Noun) Plural. Pinecones.

crèche (Noun) Nativity Scene or crib.
Oh no! Someone stole the baby Jesus from the crèche on Main Street.

cremonne [47] (Noun) A winter scarf or muffler.

crêpe [33] (Noun) A thin pancake especially good when made at camp over a wood fire.

crottes cruts [12] (Noun) Plural. Little particles found in the corners of your eyes after a long night's sleep.
Before I read the Berlin Report on Wednesday morning I have to wipe the cruts out of my eyes.

crotte de nez [23] Boogers.
Wipe that crut de nez from your face.

Crystal Falls[58] (Noun) A swimming hole in Dummer, NH.
Let's take a dip in Crystal Falls.

culottes[72] [75] (Noun) Pants. Although this is singular in standard French, it is often pluralized by French-Canadians and Franco-Americans.

dans' lune [9] (Verb) Daydreaming.

DB[39] Abbreviation for The Northland Restaurant and Dairy Bar.
Let's walk to the DB and get some ice cream.

Dead River [23] (Noun) The waterway that flows from the bog next to the high school underneath main street to the Androscoggin River, formerly a place to throw old bicycles and other trash.
Never swim in the Dead River.

deadhead[25] (Noun) Term used to described a partly submerged and difficult to see log due to the log drives in the Androscoggin River.
Lucien always carefully navigated his boat on the Androscoggin so as to avoid hitting a deadhead.

dinner and supper[52] (Noun) Dinner is lunch and supper is dinner.

dirt road, the[41] (Noun) An extension of Highland Park Avenue, which runs to 12th St Extension. Frequented by party-goers, recreational vehicle enthusiasts, and kids.
dodos or dodo[53] (Noun) A nap, typically that taken by a child.

do the groceries[70] [75] (Verb) To get groceries or to buy groceries. A French expression molded to fit English. "Faire le marché" literally "to do the market(ing) is the standard way of saying "to buy or get groceries." Some Franco-Americans say "faire les groceries."
I went to Bino and then I went to do the groceries.

douche bag (Noun) A mixture of French and English (see Franglais) meaning shower bag, travel shower kit, a bag or pouch containing toiletries and personal items.
Don't forget pack your douche bag for the trip.

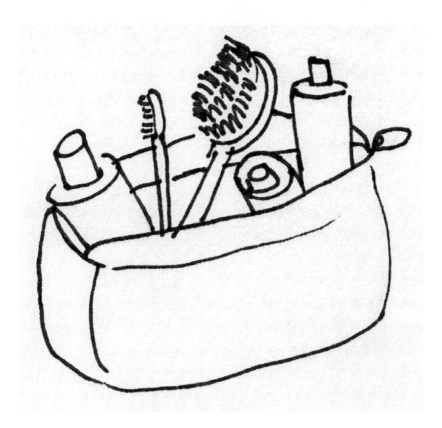

DP[23] (Abbreviation) The dirt parking lot near Berlin High School, used for smoking cigarettes and as a location for fights after school.
Meet me in the DP.

drette là, droit la[18] (Adjective) Right there.

dump, the (Noun) Referring to any place where trash is dumped legally or illegally. Commonly used to refer to Mt. Carberry Landfill in Berlin.
I kept busy shooting seagulls at the dump.

Dummer (Noun) A very small town of about 350 people to the North of Berlin.
It took Katie 40 minutes on the bus to get to school from Dummer.

dungarees[52] (Noun) Jeans.

Dunks, AKA Dunkin Donuts (Noun) A chain doughnut shop in the center of Berlin that is quite busy and frequented by regulars.
Let's go hang out at Dunks and grab a coffee.

Eagles' Field (Noun) A large empty field with a pavilion owned and operated by the Eagles Club (see the Eagles) and its members. The field is available for a variety of activities including but not limited to: bachelor parties, weddings, class reunions, graduations parties etc.
We rented out Eagles' Field and threw a great party.

Eagles, The (Noun) The Fraternal Order of Eagles or The Eagles Club. Used to refer to the actual location of the club. Membership is needed for entry.
Pierre invited us over to the Eagles tonight.

East Side [21, 50] (Noun) The area of Berlin located to the East of the Androscoggin River.

East Side Mall[41] (Noun) definition redacted in the interest of not spreading word of one of the few unplucked gems of northern NH.

Eastern Depot AKA the Depot (Noun) A restaurant and diner on the East Side of town in an old train station that serves excellent breakfast dishes and specials.
Let's go to the Depot for breakfast tomorrow.

Eeee! [63, 41, 57, 61] (Interjection) A sentence in itself. An enhancement word. Often preceding a curse word. Provides emphasis when expressing a feeling or emotion.

Eee crow![51] (Interjection) Exclamation. Popular in Berlin in the 1960s.
Eee Crow! Did you see Andre play at the Notre Dame Arena last night?

Eeh ma tante![23] (Interjection) Used to express surprise, disgust, anger, or to emphasize a statement.
Eeeh ma tante, that was a big fish!

Eh maudis! [55, 75] (Interjection) An interjection that is technically a swear meaning "Oh damn!" Also "Eh mautadit!" which means the same thing but with more emphasis.

Eh torrieu![55](Interjection) Another interjection that is less severe and is closer to damn.

l'eau blanche [49] (Noun) Bleach. Literally white water.

Elephant Mountain[22] (Noun) Another name for Mt. Forist because it looks like an elephant.

Emmanuel School of Dance (Noun) A dancing school in Berlin that every girl growing up in the 80's/90's was required to attend featuring jazz, gymnastics, ballet and tap classes that held elaborate recitals with even more elaborate costumes.

l'esprit de clocher [49] [75] (Adjective) A great love for his or her parish. Literally bell tower spirit. There's also the expression "à l'ombre du clocher" (in the shadow of the bell tower), which refers to people who tend to stay home where they feel comfortable.

étou or itou [43] Also.

face de baboune or babouin [13] (Noun) Pouting face.
The girl made a face de baboune just because she didn't get her way.

face de boeuf or beaouf [9] (Noun) Sour puss.

facelet or face laitte from face laide (Noun) A French word meaning ugly face or that is used as a term of endearment or in a teasing way.
Let's go Facelet! You're holding us up.

fesses[71, 32, 75] (Noun) The bottom or buttocks. It can be singular or plural, depending on whether one is referring to one "cheek" or both. It can also be used for meat, in the singular, as in rump. There's also the singular word "fessier" which means the whole bottom or buttocks of a person.

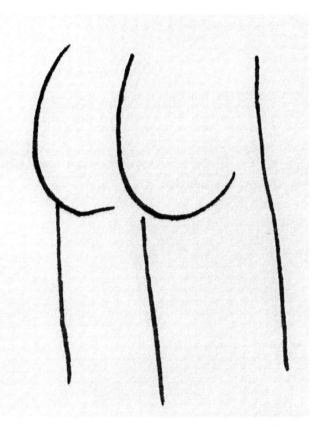

fifi [9] (Adjective) Effeminate.

figure skating (Noun) Skating using white skates with toe picks. For some time there was an organized figure skating club in Berlin.
It was difficult for her to stop since it was her first time on figure skates.

Finland Hill (Noun) A steep, almost gravity defying hill in Berlin.
My car bottomed out at the top of Finland Hill.

Flats, the [33] (Noun) See Cascade Flats.

flock mill [42] (Noun) Flock is ground and pulverized bleached cellulose (Tree fiber). The bleached wood chips were put in a large rotating drum and ground up by successively smaller and smaller ball bearings. The result was a powder like flour. This powder was used to create a felt like application for car interiors and other decorative applications. Since it was white it could be dyed to any color. The workers at the mill, being both creative and frugal, figured out that it could be substituted for flour.

Food Trend or The Trend, (Noun) A gas station and quick stop or mart centrally located on Pleasant St. Now technically an Irving, but still known as Food Trend, the spot once was a popular hangout for teens.
Let's sit out on the picnic tables at Food Trend and watch the cars go by.

Forbush Park [50] (Noun) Used when describing the neighborhoods of Berlin to describe the area near Forbush St.

Forum, The (Noun) A morning call-in radio program on AM 1230 hosted by Bob Barbin that featured local news, interviews, and rants by callers.
Did you hear Mon Oncle Fred on the Forum yesterday?

foufouns [4] (Noun) Meaning a baby's butt.

four by twice[42] (Noun) A 2 x 4 piece of lumber.
Rollie went up to White Mountain Lumber to get 6 four by twices.

Franglais[41] (Noun) An English/French hybrid language once prominent throughout the city, and now generally only heard in certain places, such as King's School aka "the East Side Mall."

French mass (Noun) The Catholic Mass that was held in French at Angel Guardian in Berlin. It was known to be 15 minutes shorter than English Mass.
It was a family tradition to attend French Mass on Christmas Eve.

fricassée[9] (Noun) In Berlin, a ground beef and potato soup.

Friday night skating (Noun) Open skating or recreational skating at the Notre Dame Arena in which mostly unattended children skate in circles for two hours.
Colette and Frank had their first date at Friday Night Skating.

Fyshy Cocktail [23] (Noun) An alcoholic beverage made with Hawaiian Punch, pink lemonade, and vodka.
I could use a Fyshy Cocktail right about now.

galendor [49] (Noun) Two person saw.

Gamm (Noun) An industrial park in Berlin with several businesses with a large parking lot.
I learned to drive up at Gamm.

'gâre-la donc, gâr ladon, regarde la donc[18][75] (Verb) Look at her! Can be used in the positive sense as in a nice looking woman and also in the negative sense as in "Who does she think she is?"

gaz[70] (Noun) Gasoline.
I filled my car with gaz so I would make it to Walmarts.

ginnig, guénigue, ganig [28, 44, 3, 75] (Noun) Blanket or rag, raggy, or towel that is old and worn. Derived from guénille.

go downstreet [74] (Noun) To go downtown.

Gold House (Noun) A local pizza shop and restaurant serving Greek style food with especially thinly sliced peppers.
We picked up our order, number 18, at Gold House.

gonflé, gonfil [59] (Adjective) To be full from eating.

good 'n you? [70] An expression and automatic response. Also seen in several variations on vanity license plates.
So how are you this morning Rosaire? Goodnyou?

Gorham (Noun) The town south of Berlin where all of the fast food chains are. The Second part of the BG road lies there. The relationship between the city of Berlin and the town of Gorham could be described as brotherly.
Let's head down to Gorham for the 4th of July Carnival.

got her baby [70] (Verb) To have a baby or give birth.
She got her baby last week Tuesday.

Le Grand Bois du Nord [23] (Noun) The Great North Woods, the greatest place on Earth.
Bienvenue au Grand Bois du Nord!

Granite Curtain (Noun) The Granite Curtain refers to the phenomenon of living above the Notches (see the Notch). This theory was developed in the early 2000s as explanation for many anomalies that occur in Berlin.

The notches serve as a blockade that inhibits the flow of goods and services to the North Country. In this way, it is similar to the Iron Curtain, however the Granite Curtain division is geological and not political.

The rugged terrain creates a time lag between the North Country and the rest of the world that is estimated to be about 7 years. The time lag affects things like fashion, news, and music.

Dude, did Starter Jackets just hit up here? Yeah, it's the Granite Curtain.

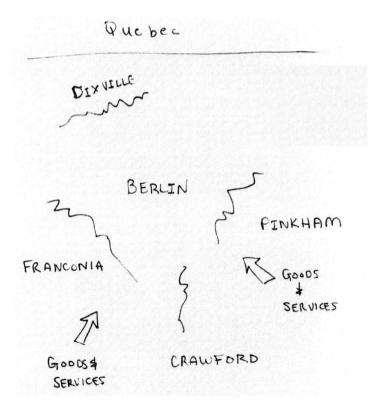

graveyard[40] (Noun) A mixture of all of the types of soda at the Notre Dame Arena. Graveyards may also be made from Slush Puppy at the Big Apple.
The little boy made a graveyard at the Notre Dame Arena.

Green Front, the[21] (Noun) This was the name used for the State Liquor store that used to be located on Pleasant Street. It was painted green and that's where the name originated. This was an alternate name used to refer to the liquor store so others (especially children) wouldn't know where you were going.

Green Street (Noun) A very small park near the police station and recreation center that is used for youth soccer but is most well-known for the outdoor ice rink that is created during the winter.
Wow, this ice is so bumpy it's like Green Street in here.

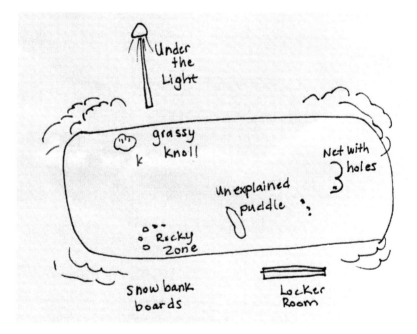

Greetings Jewelers, (Noun) Hall of Greetings, Hallmark. A Main Street shop with high-end items, gifts, jewelry and greeting cards.
Look at this finely wrapped present; it must be from the Hall of Greetings.

grill candy [23] (Noun) Steak marinated in a secret recipe only available from Rudy's, a Berlin favorite.
I am craving grill candy right now.

grouille-toé [49] (Verb) Move yourself.

grutone or gortons [42 75] (Noun) Ground pork that was also a breakfast meat spread that is not appealing to the eye but is very tasty.

have a tree [74] At Christmas time, instead of putting up a tree or getting a tree.

hice [26] (Noun) Ice.

homeworks (Noun) homework as said by a French speaker. This type of pluralization can be applied to many words for example Internets.
My grandmother offered to help me with my homeworks.

horseshoes AKA shoes (Noun) A yard game enjoyed by all types of folks the goal of which is to throw a horseshoe as close to a pin as possible.
I just finished mowing the lawn. Want to play a game of shoes?

Horne Field [1] (Noun) A field across from Brown school for Norwegian village children to play in

Horne Field Stonehenge [41] (Noun) When God made Berlin he left his handprint·on a large rock. This rock is part of a formation of rocks; one of which serves well as a bed to gaze into the heavens.

Hutchins Park (Noun) A public park on the East Side of Berlin on Hutchins St.
Let's sled down the slide into the snow bank at Hutchins Park.

I was to [74] A way of describing travel.
I was to Concord yesterday.

IGA (I-G-A) (eh-gee-a) **or IGGA** (Noun) Independent Grocers Association store in Berlin on Glen Ave with everything you need including local specialties including chili bits, whoopee pies and Bulldog sauce. There also was Prince's then Steve's IGA on Pleasant St.
I've got to stop at the IGGA to for some scratch tickets and whoopie pies.

il mouille [49] It's raining. Literally it is wetting.

Irish Acres [21, 50] (Noun) Used to describe the neighborhood of Berlin immediately surrounding St. Kieran's Church and St. Patrick's school that was originally settled by Irish immigrants.

Jericho [50] (Noun) The area of Berlin located near Jericho Lake including Jericho Road.

Joliette Snowshoe Club (Noun) A local fraternal order with a bar and waterhole for members only. Formerly on the corner of Mason and Pleasant St.
We headed over to the Snowshoe Club for a quick drink.

Jump, the. [33] (Noun) See Nansen Ski Jump.

Jungle, the [33] (Noun) Located near the railroad tracks off Glen Avenue where a lot of homeless and desperate people made their home.

Kentucky Fried Chicken (Noun) Located across from the Notre Dame Arena, the locally owned franchise sold not only chicken but also Berlin photographs, postcards and memorabilia.
I bet you she can eat 7 Chicken Littles at Kentucky Fried Chicken.

kestufalà qu'est tu fa' là? qu'est ce que tu fais la? [18] What are you doing there?

King's School (Noun) See East Side Mall.

kossé, cossé? Qu'est ce que c'est?[18] What?

Kushi Kato [39] (Noun) A rectangular block of chicken fried on a stick with onion and green pepper.
I had two kushi with my fried rice last night.

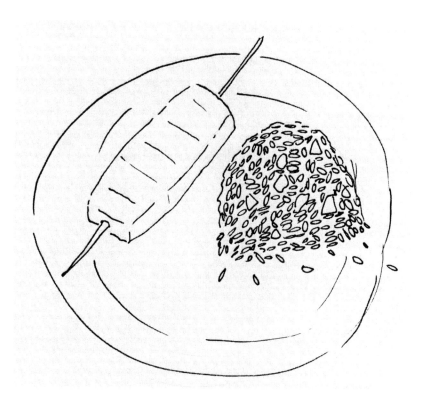

Labonville (Noun) A local company specializing in outdoor gear, clothing and equipment.
Every logger in the North Country wears Labonville's pants.

lampe[72] (Noun) Lamp.

Laverdiere's (Noun) A New England chain drug store and general store on Pleasant St in Berlin. Now Rite Aid number two.

leader[3] (Noun) Extension cord.
Fred couldn't finish his new addition without a longer leader.

lève ta savate [49][75] Lift up your feet. Literally lift your shoe. Savate is an old worn out shoe.

Level 10 (Noun) A band from Berlin that specialized in rock/pop music and was a staple at special events including weddings, proms, etc.
I saw Level 10 at the band stand at Super Sunday.

Liberty Park [21] [50] (Noun) The area in the northern section of the East Side where the streets are named after World War I generals and locations. For example, Pershing Ave., Rheims Street and Verdun Street.

Little Berlin (Noun) A settlement of camps (see camps) along the Magoloway River and the parts of Lake Umbagog. See up the river.
Priscilla's family has a camp up at Little Berlin.

log drive [25] (Noun) The act of floating logs down a river to a pulp mill rather than transportation over land.
My pépère loved to reminisce about the massive log drives of the Brown Paper Company clogging the Androscoggin.

Manchester Union (Noun) The Manchester Union Leader Newspaper
I love reading the Manchester Union every morning with my coffee

mange du naveau [49] Eat some turnip.

maringouin [3, 75] (Noun) From the Native American word for Mosquito.

Mary's [21,33] (Noun) Mary's Pizza Place in Cascade, a long standing and immensely popular place to eat in Cascade Flats.

ma tante or matante [56] (Noun) My Aunt.
I went to go see my Ma Tante Diane at work.

maquereau or macreau [9] [75] (Noun) a playboy. Also means pimp. Also means mackerel as in the fish.

Meat pie, or **Tourtière** (Noun) A savory dinner pie made of meat, usually pork, beef or a combination of both with potatoes and spices including clove.
My Mémère made 12 meat pies *for Christmas.*

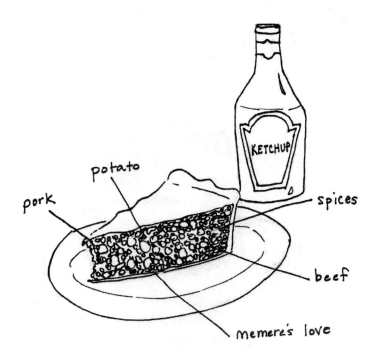

pork

potato

spices

beef

memere's love

Mel's Arcade (Noun) A small arcade on Main St. owned by a guy named Mel.
My mom said I can only spend one dollar at Mel's Arcade.

Mémère[43] (Noun) Grandmother. Variations include but ar not limited to Mem, Mémé, Mimi, grandmère.
My Mémère took me to me to church and then to the Dairy Bar.

Memorial Field (Noun) A field and baseball formerly used by Berlin High School for field hockey, soccer and other events. Memorial Field Annex is across from this field and houses recreational softball games.
Kayla has a ten o'clock game at the Annex. Homeruns are few and far between at Memorial Field.

Mets ça sur la corniche [49] Put that on the shelf.

Mets de l'eau dans la bombe [49] Fill the kettle water, put water in the kettle.

Mets la soupe sur le poêle[49, 75] To start dinner. Literally to put the soup on the stove.

Milan (Noun) A small town/village north of Berlin with farms, fields and friends. Flatlanders pronounce it Me-lan, as in Italy.
We rode up to Milan to go fishing.

Milan Luncheonette (Noun) A greasy spoon diner with specials and many types of food.
Pick up some pizza and chicken fingers at the Luncheonette on your way home.

Millyard, the (Noun) 1. The area nearby and around the Berlin Mills in which chips, logs and trucks were stored. 2. A bar located on the East Side serving affordable drinks with simple décor including a mirrored mural of Berlin also known as the Yard.
1. The trucks pulled into the millyard and swept off the extra woodchips.
2. Eventually, Scott needed to be shut off at the Millyard.

minou minew [3, 70, 37, 9, 41] (Noun) A cat.
My minou coughs up hairballs all of the time.

Ming House/China Inn (Noun) A Chinese restaurant located on Hillside Ave near the Notre Dame Arena. Formerly the China Inn. See Red Sauce.

Robert ordered a #11 and red sauce at the China Inn.

minous [71] (Noun) The fuzz between your toes. See also mousse. See also minou.

la mitaine [16] (Noun) The Protestant church that also served as a meeting house where people gathered for functions or for prayer. When the English took over Canada and started building their own meeting houses, the French Canadians called them "mitaines," a corruption of the word "meeting." Priests forbade their parishioners to enter a "mitaine."

moé or moué [49] (Pronoun) Me.

mon chou [49, 9, 75] (Noun) My darling. Literally my cabbage. The feminine version is "ma chouette" literally, my barn owl.

Mona's Restaurant [33] (Noun) A well-known restaurant in Cascade Flats, before the time of Mary's. Catered to the men working shifts at the Cascade Mill. The restaurant stood right near the front entrance of the Cascade Paper Mill, and was run by Mona and Arthur Corriveau.

Monaco to Jericho [23] A phrase used by coaches in the 70's to tell Berlin High hockey players to skate from one end of the rink to the other.

Mon Oncle or mon onc' [44, 56] (Noun) My uncle or uncle.
Mon Oncle Dick is having a bbq Tuesday night.

moose (Noun) Large mammals with extremely low intelligence that live in swamps, wooded areas and wander out into busy roads.
We drove up to Success Loop to look for Moose.

Moose Meadow The Meadow, Moose Ghetto (Noun) A mini golf course and arcade in Gorham NH frequented by teens and young adults.
Ready to play a round of putt-putt at Moose Meadow?

mouche (Noun) A fly but also any pest or general annoyance.
Ahhh, get out of my face mouche!

mousse, moussie [17, 3, 73, 28, 23, 43] (Noun) Lint, dust bunnies, fuzz balls.
Clean the moussies out from under the couch.
You have a mousse on your sweater.

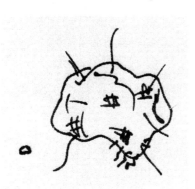

Mt. Jasper (Noun) A small mountain behind Berlin High School with a view of Berlin and caves. Arrowheads made by Native Americans were found in the caves and can be seen at the Berlin Public library.

We climbed up Mt. Jasper during science class as part of a nature walk.

muddin' (Noun) Driving trucks with obscenely large tires in the mud also driving smaller recreational vehicles in the mud. Often the trucks must be towed out. See also mud season.

Dennis went muddin' with his buddies.

mud season (Noun) The season after winter and before summer during the months of later March, April and May.
The truck got stuck on the dirt road during Mud Season.

Muckaluck [29] A chainsaw, specifically a McCulloch chain saw. McCullochs were one of the more popular saws with professional loggers from the 1950s through the 1980s.

murals (Noun) Painted murals depicting scenes from Berlin's history and culture on the walls of buildings in alleys on Main St.
We helped paint the ski jump on the mural in the alley.

Napert Village [50] (Noun) The neighborhood of Berlin that was/is in the shadow of the Mill. Located off of Hutchins Street including the streets Napert St. and Gauthier St.

Nansen Ski Jump (Noun) Built in 1936, the jump was one of the tallest on the East Coast. It was home to Olympic Trials and Regional Championships. The jump is 170 feet tall and approximately 260 feet long. The angle of descent is approximately 37.5 degrees. The last jumps were held in the 1980s. (1988) See also Sideways.
She often talks about watching the ski jumpers at Nansen. We went sledding at the base of the Ski Jump.

Natty Light (Noun) Natural Light Beer, a popular beverage that is cheap and readily available. See also the Pastures.
Pick up a sixer of Natty Light before you head to the party.

Narrows, the [21] (Noun) The area of town along north Main Street where the numbered streets are. This area had narrow, closely placed streets.

Naveau navet or [3] (Noun) A holiday dish of carrots and turnips.

NCHL (Noun) North Country Hockey League, an adult hockey league that features a high level of play with a devout local following.
The NCHL championships are tomorrow night.

Nibrocs (Noun) Brown paper hand towels invented by Corbin and manufactured at the Berlin Mills.

ninune[43] (Noun) A foolish person.

noisette[49] Not too smart, you're nuts. Literally a hazel nut.

Northern Lights (Noun) A building and housing units on Main Street in Berlin for senior citizens. Formerly St. Regis hospital.
Jeanette's mom moved into Northern Lights

Northland Restaurant and Dairy Bar (Noun) A popular Berlin restaurant featuring fried fish, seafood and American style entrees. Known for the dessert menu including ice cream especially whips, frappes, and fruit pies.

Norwegian Village [21, 33, 50] (Noun) The area north and west of Brown School that was originally settled by people of Scandinavian heritage. The streets include Sweden, Denmark, Finland, and Norway Street. Also called Scandinavian Village.

Notch, the (Noun) Referring to any notch (ie Pinkham Notch, Crawford Notch, Dixville Notch etc) The Notch is a geological formation that cuts through a mountainous area. The phrase The Notch usually refers to roads that cut through the mountains. See also Granite Curtain theory.
The weather was so terrible I couldn't make it through the Notch. The winds picked up, the sky was gray and it began snowing as soon as we entered, the Notch.

Notre Dame Arena (Noun) See also the Arena. The ice arena on Hillside Avenue in Berlin. Home to Berlin Youth Hockey, Friday Night Skating, Berlin High Hockey, Broomball, NCHL and now Spartan's Weightlifting.

obedon or au bedon [31, 44] A shortcut for "ou bien...donc." Meaning "either this...or that...thus..."

Old Notre Dame (School) (Noun) A catholic high school located on School Street. The school was closed in 1972 and recent efforts have lead to the salvage of the building.
I drove by the Old Notre Dame school and saw that they had boarded up the windows.

ongle [72] (Noun) Fingernail.

open the light [8] (Verb) To turn on the light. See also close the light.

ôte toé de d'la, ote toi de la [18] Get out of there.

oyons [31] (Interjection) Omitting the V from Voyons. Meaning "Come on!" uttered in a spirit of disbelief.

pain de fesses (Noun) A loaf of bread that looks like a pair of buttocks especially Canadian bread.

pare a cinquante [56] Speed up.

pass the mop [68] (Verb) to mop the floor.

Pastures, the (Noun) See Natty Light. See dirt road. See the water tower.

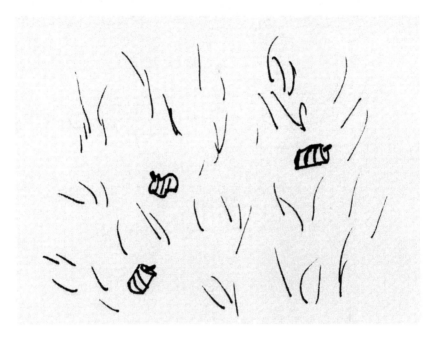

pâtè chinois [65] See Chinese pie.

Patio, the (Noun) The covered and paved area outside of the cafeteria at Berlin High School where smoking was permitted until the 90s. *Dude, lets go smoke some butts, there, out on the patio.*

Peak FM (Noun) A radio station based out of Conway NH that played pop music.
We called Peak FM to request our favorite Richard Marx song.

Penney's or Pennies (Noun) JC Penney.
Did you use your coupon at the sale at Penney's?

Pépère (Noun) Grandfather also Pep Grandpere, etc.
Pépère shoveled snow for 2 hours yesterday before coming inside.

petauer [24] (Adjective) A word used to describe fire-crackers.

pettes de la soeur [60] (Noun) A dessert that is made with left over pie crust. The dough is rolled flat, buttered, covered with brown sugar, baked then sliced to look like a pinwheel. Literally my sister's farts.

Petit Canada [50] (Noun) Area of Berlin including Pine, Willow, State, Park Sts., especially near the bottom of Willow St.

pi, et puis [18] What's new?

Piche Nut also pistchnotte or pichenotte (Noun) (Verb) 1. A French-Canadian table game with 4 pockets and open round discs that are flicked into the corners, using the hands, for points. 2. To flick someone or something using the method of placing the index finger on the thumb as done in the game of Piche Nut.

1.We played seven games of Piche Nut during our Christmas Eve tournament.

2. Emma stop piche nutting your sister in the ear.

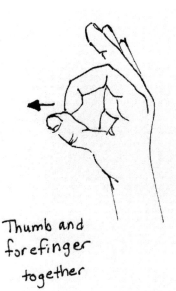

Thumb and
forefinger
together

Release in an
upward flicking
motion

pichous [23, 70, 55] (Noun) A knitted slipper. Variations in other Franco-American communities include chaussure and pantoufle.

My mémère knit everyone in my family a pair of pichous for Christmas.

pied à fesses (Adjective) To run with your feet hitting your butt, often done by children.

pique-pique [13] (Noun) pick-pick. A slang word meaning a burr or picky part of a plant.

pissenlit [59] (Noun) a dandelion. Literally piss on the ground.

piton [8,23,41,51] (Noun) any kind of button that you push. Could also be used to desribe a peg.
Push the piton to turn on the TV; the hockey game is on!

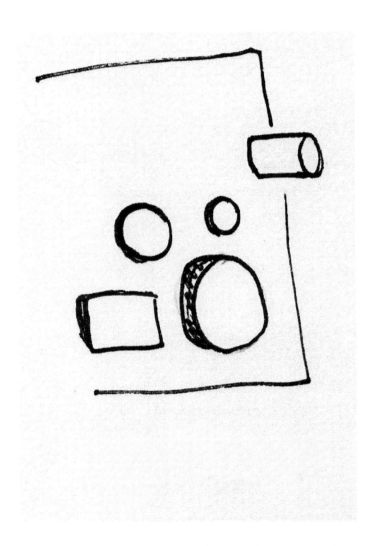

pitonne[36] (Noun) a truck full of uncut lumber.
Once again, we found ourselves behind a pitonne on a no-passing road.

pitou or pitounne[12, 43, 68] (Noun) 1 a little sweetheart. 2. a penis.
My memere always says, "Its so good to see my little pitou." The toddler kept telling everyone he knew where his pitou was.

plaster[11] (Noun) bandaid.
I need a plaster for my boo-boo.

plastic rain bonnet (Noun) A rain bonnet made of plastic that is worn by women to prevent the hair from getting wet after it has been set.

My mémère always carries her rain bonnet.

FOLDS
UP
SMALL

Extends to
Protect recently
Set hair.

Transparent, Floral and colors
available

Pontook Dam (Noun) A dam (See Up the River) that is a popular spot for recreational activities such as fishing, ice fishing and paddling.

Pool Room [33] (Noun) located in downtown Berlin, on Main St. where, especially on Friday nights, when the shops were open until 9pm, the young men would stand outside and "watch the girls go by,"

Portland Hill (Noun) A closed off portion of road that connected Church St to Prospect St. It is currently barricaded and overgrown but still used as a walking short cut.
Let go up Portland Hill, it's steeper but shorter.

porta potat [53] (Noun) A closet or area typically in a cellar that was formerly used to store vegetables and other food items that don't belong in the refrigerator.

le porte dur or porte-ordures [13] [75] (Noun) Dust pan. In this context, "porte" is used as a verb, "[to] carry" combined with a noun, "ordures" is yet another word for garbage, filth, etc. So, when put together with a hyphen, it becomes a noun that literally it means "carry garbage" or "carry filth."

pouèvre [72] (Noun) Pepper.

poutine [39, 23] (Noun) French fries served with brown gravy and cheese curd on top.
I ordered some poutine at the Valley Creek Eatery.

Princess Theater (Noun) A movie theater in Berlin on Main Street that has changed ownership, been closed and reopened over the years.
The girls went to the Princess to see Harry Potter.

Pub, the. Fagin's Pub (Noun) A popular Irish pub on Main Street in Berlin. Recently destroyed by fire.
The night before Thanksgiving is my favorite night at the Pub. To the Pub!

pup-corn [66] (Noun) Popcorn pronounced with the emphasis on 1st syllable, as in the shapes of some exploded kernels that resemble little pups. Said with great affection for the product.

put out the lights [26] (Verb) To turn off the lights. See also open and close the lights.

quesse tuveux ksam fasse, qu'est ce que tu veux que ca me fasse? [18] Do you think I care?

quette [4,67,70] (Noun) An unruly piece or section of hair.
Your quette is so out of control I can't see past your head.

ragou [9] (Noun) French stew with cloves.

Rainbow Shop, the [41] (Noun) Small mid-80s store located in the JC Penney block, which supplied Berlin with rock music and related merchandise: pins, bandanas, back patches, etc. It also carried pipes, knives, nunchucks, and Chinese throwing stars.

Ramsey Hill [50] (Noun) The Ramsey Street neighborhood of Berlin at the top of Hillside Ave.

Rec Center, the (Noun) The main offices of the Berlin Recreation Department located on Green St and First Ave featuring a gymnasium where elementary basketball, dances, jazzercise and line dancing take place.
The Third and Fourth grade basketball championships were held at the Rec Center.

Red Sauce (Noun) Served at the China Inn. Pineapple juice, vinegar, red number 5 and sugar.
I'd like extra red sauce with that please.

Regarder si c'est pas beau ca? [5] Isn't that something or isn't that beautiful?

Rendezvous du Roi [59] (Noun) A restaurant in Berlin that was very popular with young and old alike. See also tunaburger.

Res, the (Noun) A reservoir of water. Located at the end of Burgess St. on the southern end of the East Side.
Let's go hang out by the Res.

Rich, the [70] (Noun) Rich's Department Store.
I used to love to shop at the Rich all the time before it closed.

riggin [44] (Noun) A gadget.

river rats [34] (Noun) Seagulls that are found along the Androscoggin River.

roost [41] (Verb) A word with a wide variance of use, usually suggesting a display of awesome, reckless, aggressiveness.

Rudy's Market (Noun) Originally corner store and deli now a butcher shop located on Wight St. See also grill candy.
I think Tom is in the backroom at Rudy's.

Russian Church (Noun) A Russian Orthodox
Church in Berlin known for its striking onion top
architecture and prominence in the Berlin skyline.
Sam lives over by the Russian Church.

sadlairàsah, Ca a l'air de [18] It looks that way.

salvage [33] (Noun) An employment pool run by Brown Company and where the men without steady jobs would check in every day for work.

Sanborn, the (Noun) A music venue in Berlin adjacent to the Bodyline built in an old barn, a popular hang out in up until the 90s when it closed. See 8084.
It's BYOB at the Sanborn.

sand pits or the Pits (Noun) Sand dunes and pits behind the Berlin High School often used recreationally for ATV's and dirt bikes.
Run to the Pits and back for a warm-up.

Sari-sari Shop, the [41] (Noun) A late 80s business in downtown Berlin that sold everything you could imagine, and would sell it to whomever wished for it.

scatain [23] (Adjective) Dirty, gross, repulsive.
Don't let the dog in the house, she's all scatain!

scroggin' [41] (Verb) To have sex.
Yeah, Carol and I have been together for 8 months now, and I think, if I remember correctly, I first scrogged her up at the res after we saw 8084 play at the Joliette.

scunion [69] (Noun) A scallion.

Seven Islands Bridge (Noun) A bridge on the Androscoggin up the river that is a common swimming area and more commonly a jumping area.
I dare you to jump off the Seven Islands Bridge.

Sherbrooke (Noun) A small city in Canada that is accessible and relatively short distance away from Berlin featuring clubs, bars and depending on the dollar, cheap hockey equipment.
Don't tell Mom I am going to Sherbrooke tonight to go dancing.

side by each [70] To line up or arrange side by side.
The teacher instructed the students to line up side by each.

sideways [64] (Noun) A nickname was actually the Nansen Wayside park across from the Nansen ski jump.

Sinibaldi's[33] (Noun) See also Millyard. An Italian restaurant on the East Side of Berlin featuring a variety of original cuisine and adaptations of other local favorites including poutine and kushi. They often run steak specials and other affordable deals.
Our whole family headed to Sinibaldi's for my Ma Tante's birthday.

Skatey Kat (Noun) A roller skating rink in Milan NH.
Sheila loved to play 4 corners and limbo at Skatey Kat.

Ski-do (Noun or Verb) A snowmobile or to ride a snow mobile. See also snow machine. This also refers to an outfit worn during the wintertime i.e. ski-do pants or ski-do suit.
We went Ski-doing up on the trails at Jericho.
Ben wore his ski-do suit to go skiing.

skidder (Noun) Large four-wheel drive machine by loggers to skid logs out of the woods. It also used as a landscaping tool. Variations include grapple and cable.
After Michael's truck broke through the ice we used a skidder to pull it out.

slaq a quarante[56] Slow down.

sliding [41] (Verb) Berlin equivalent of what the rest of the world incorrectly knows as sledding. Since it is winter 6 months of the year in Berlin, we are the authority on this.

smoke stacks or the Stacks (Noun) The smoke stacks on the Berlin Mill.
I couldn't believe the Stacks were imploded. Did you see the Christmas tree on the stacks?

snow day (Noun) This is a mythical concept that school would be closed when it snows. This does not exist in Berlin although it appears to be practiced in other areas of the state. It is elusive, like a unicorn and has rumored to have only happened twice in the history of Berlin Public Schools.
Let's watch TV to see if we have a snow day. Nope. What's a snow day Mommy?

snowmachine [23, 52] (Noun) A vehicle used for traveling on snow, known as a snowmobile elsewhere.
I'm going to ride my snowmachine tomorrow.

sodee or sody[20, 45] (Noun) A cola, soda pop or soft drink.

sour de sire [52] (Noun) A candy in was available in Berlin.

South Pond (Noun) A pond and recreational area in Stark NH with swimming, barbeque and playground areas
The sun is shining and we're heading up to South Pond for the day.

St. Anne Church (Noun) A very large Roman Catholic church in Berlin made of red brick with an ornate interior. The prominent steeple is a key feature to the Berlin skyline.
They got a new relic at St. Anne Church.

St. Gilles[50] (Noun) A neighborhood in the Granite St. Mason St., bottom of School St. area of Berlin. Granite St used to be called St. Gilles, named for the region where most of the French-Canadians in that area came from.

Stark (Noun) A small town north of Milan of about 500 people and known for its covered bridge. See South Pond.
We drove through Stark on our way to Groveton.

Store, the[1] (Noun) In the early 50s there was a neighborhood grocery store, on upper Main Street, just north of Brown School. Neighborhood children referred to it as "The Store."

Success (Noun) A township West of Berlin that is inhabited mostly by seasonal residents and is used for recreational purposes including shooting, etc.
I took my 4 wheela up to Success for a ride.

Success Loop (Noun) A road in Milan that formerly looped around a wetland/swampy area that was a home to moose and other creatures.
Moose Tours go up around Success Loop and use a light to help spot the moose.

Super Sunday (Noun) A parade, festival and event held in downtown Berlin during the 1980s that featured contests, street vendors and music. Youngsters often ran wild spraying silly string and being mischievous.
My cousins won the bike-decorating contest in the Super Sunday parade.

swamp donkeys [23] (Noun) Moose.
Watch out for swamp donkeys when you're driving.

Swap Shop (Noun) A radio call-in show and flea market on AM1230.
I sold my old armoire on Swap Shop.

swetteur [46] (Noun) Sweater.
Mets ton swetteur. Put your sweater on.

T n C (Noun) The Town and Country Motor Inn, hotel, restaurant and function hall in Gorham NH that holds weddings, dances and other special events. With live music and comedy nights it is also a venue for entertainment.
Our class reunion was held at the T n C.

ta tu d'javusah, as tu jamais vu ca? [18] Can you believe it.

Tabernac (Noun) Curse word literally meaning the tabernacle, the area that holds the hosts in the church. Actual definition is more colorful.
Tabernac! Ouch that hurts!

Tabarnoush, Tahbanoosh[23, 51] (Interjection) A gentler and made-up derivative of cursing on the "Tabernacle."
I smashed my thumb with a hammer; eeeh tabar noush!

tagging (Verb) A sanctioned and acceptable means of begging for money by standing outside of local business establishments with paper cups asking patrons to support Youth Hockey or Little League or what have you.
I made $37.29 tagging at the IGA.

tanker or tankay[5] (Noun) Car, automobile.

tatones[35] (Noun) Boobs.

Tech, the (Noun) New Hampshire Technical College at Berlin, Berlin Technical College, White Mountains Community College. The Community/Technical College in Berlin on Riverside Drive offering many different programs and courses including culinary arts, teacher prep and early childhood education, IT, nursing, and automotive programs among others.
Ray just graduated from the Tech.

le temps se chagrine[49] It's getting cloudy or the weather is gloomy. Literally the weather is becoming depressed.

tenet or tanant (Noun) A pest or brat or overall annoying person.
Hey tenet, stop poking me.

Tete-de-pioche or **tight piosh**[65,14] (Adjective) Stubborn or hard-headed.
He's a tight piosh.

toé[49] (pronoun) You.

Tombola [2, 41] (Noun) A yearly celebration which took place in the Guardian Angel School parking lot, featuring carnival rides, bingo, and related fanfare.

Did you see Amy barf all over the place on the Zipper at the Tombola? I wore my new sweatpants to the Tombola.

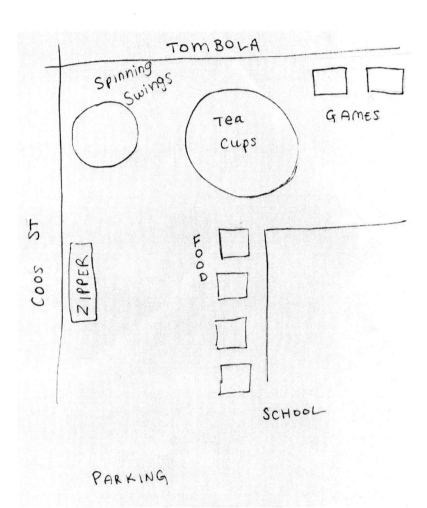

Tondreau parking lot (Noun) Tondreau Park and parking lot are city parks along the Androscoggin River behind City Hall.
Michelle, Tim and Dennis are hanging out in the Tondreau parking lot.

torchon [44] (Noun) A rung out rag.

touk or **tuque** [19, 58] (Noun) A knitted hat you wear in the winter.

tourcaire [72] (Noun) See also meat pie.

towel room (Noun) A section of the Berlin Mills were paper towels were made.
Roland picked up another shift at the Towel room for Monday nights.

tramp, the (Noun) A trampoline on Hillside Avenue where any child could jump if they were familiar with the rules of the tramp.

> The first rule of the tramp is that there is no tramp
> Second Rule: Only two people at a time
> Third Rule: No back flips

tree [62] (Noun-cardinal number) Three.
We drive to Gorham to da Rich to buy two, tree, maybe five tings

Treasure Kit (Noun) A large and unwieldy cardboard box of items for sale as a school fundraiser that was carried from door-to-door by small children as they attempted to sell sponges, gift wrap and magnets to their neighbors and relatives. There was only one way the items could fit properly into the box and once they were removed it took approximately 30 minutes to reconfigure and arrange the items so that the box would close.

The handle broke on my Treasure Kit, spilling the contents all over the street.

trow [62] (Verb) To throw.
Trow me down da stairs my sweater me.

true [26] (Preposition and adverb) Through
Don't cut true my yard, go around!

tu me crétu?, me crois-tu?[18] Do you believe me?

tunaburger [64] (Noun) It was a house specialty at Norm's Family Drive In, later called, Le Rendezvous du Roi. It is a deep fried tuna fish sandwich made on a bun, coated with bread crumbs similar to onion rings and the true recipe is a secret.

tunnel, the at St Patrick's school (Noun) A dark tunnel in the basement of St. Patrick's school (also BRCS and St Michael's) that went from one end of the school to the other. Possibly a fall-out shelter.
Although it was against the rules, I had to run in the tunnel.

twinkies [33] (Noun) A famous ice cream novelty made at Emma's Restaurant and they were always ready on Sunday afternoon.

'tsig guy or 'tit guy [35] (Noun) Slang or nickname for small man.

UBCU Jacket (Noun) A blue windbreaker jacket that was given away for free to members of the United Brotherhood Credit Union. This item quickly became the most popular article of clothing in the city and could be seen anywhere and everywhere since it is wrong to turn down a free jacket.

We looked out at church to a sea of blue, nearly 95 percent of the congregation was wearing a UBCU Jacket.

Mike wore his UBCU Jacket everyday for three years.

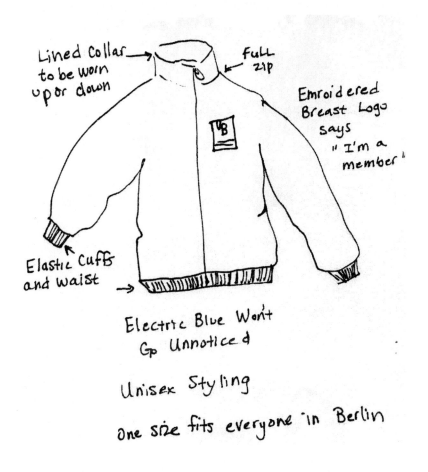

Lined Collar
to be worn
up or down

full
zip

Emroidered
Breast Logo
says
" I'm a
member "

Elastic Cuffs
and waist

Electric Blue Won't
Go Unnoticed

Unisex Styling

One size fits everyone in Berlin

up the river (Noun)/(Verb) A location, any location North of Berlin. Also the verb tense to go up the river.
Stacey headed up the river for the weekend.

upstairs (at Middle Earth) (Noun) The adult section of the popular downtown store in the 'Shire.
We ventured Upstairs at Middle Earth.

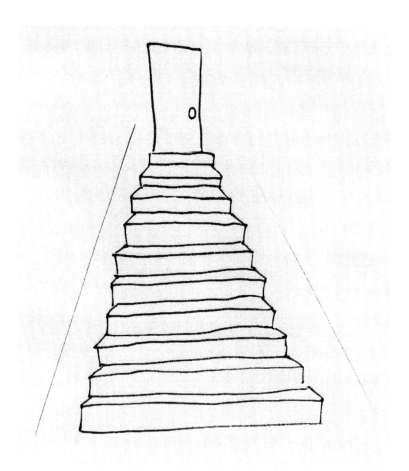

va à la potiquerre [49] (Verb) To go to the drugstore or pharmacy.

va acheter de la carasine [49] (Verb) To go buy some kerosene.

va te choucher [49] You're kidding. Literally go to bed.

vatendon, vas t'en donc [18] You're kidding me.

vinegar white vinegar (Noun) A condiment to put on french fries.
At the Arena, she dosed her french fries in vinegar.

Vinkerville [30] (Noun) This was a slang word for the area where most of the people from Norway, Sweden, Finland etc lived.

Voyons or Voyon donc [9] (Interjection) Oh come on! Also yeah right!
Voyon! That's ridiculous!

Walmarts [70] (Noun) A "big box" retailer in Gorham NH.
They have everything there at the WalMarts but I liked the Rich better.

water tower, the [41] (Noun) A popular location for high school parties in the late 80s and 90s located between the dirt road and the pasture.

West Side [50] (Noun) A less used name for the side of the town that lies to the West of the Androscoggin River. This term is less popular than the "East Side" which refers to the area of the city to the East of the river. Often used ironically to reference Hip Hop culture ie West Siiide.
Most of our friends lived on the West Side.

WBRL [41] (Noun) Famous Berlin radio station found at 1400 AM on your dial. Provided Berlin with great rock music up until the early 80's via colorful DJ's such as "Charlie in the

Morning," who once rode an elephant in a parade in Gorham
NH.

Where are you going, you? [17] A question in English with
French structure.
whip [20](Noun) Soft serve ice cream.

wicked[19](Adjective) Meaning very or strongly.
I heard you got a wicked good job.

wiggamagig [43](Noun) Object or thingiedo.

WOKQ (Noun) Country radio station in Berlin.
Have you heard the new Shania song on WOKQ?

wood chip pile (Noun) The very large pile of wood chips
that formed a soft mountain in the Millyard on the East Side.
It would be so cool to sled down the wood chip pile.

Woyondon[4] See voyons.

yinque, rien que[18] Only.

Yokohama or the Yoko (Noun) See also Kushi Kato. A
Japanese/American restaurant in Gorham NH known for
fried rice, Kushi, Bulldog Sauce and Mai Thais. Bootleg
copies of recipes are floating around that attempt to reveal
the secret ingredients in the food.
My family went to the Yoko for my parent's anniversary dinner.

List of Contributors

1. **Adair, Ken.** *Bark field, Horne field, 1st-7th Holes, The Store.*
2. **Aube, Justin.** *Tombola.*
3. **Aube, Jerry and Jill.** *gingue, leader, mardagin, minew, mouss, navu.*
4. **Barr, Lucille.** *foufons, quette, woyondons.*
5. **Beaudoin, Beatrice.** *Caoutchou, regarder c'est pas beau cà, tankay.*
6. **Beaudoin, Claude.** *Berlin.*
7. **Bellefeuille, Francis "Frank."** *ca c'est une coureuse, ca c'est une gasse, je vais en fall.*
8. **Bergeron, Dave.** *open/close the lights, piton.*
9. **Bergeron, René.** *barbotte, boude, boudin, caribou, ce fais encroire, choo, cochon, dans la lune, face de beaouf, fifi/tapette, fricassee, macreau, minew,*
10. **Berube, Rachel.** *aller à fall.*
11. **Blais, Dan and Darlene.** *plaster.*
12. **Blais, David.** *bonhomme, crahuts, peetoo.*
13. **Blais, Muriel.** *aller à fall, face de babouin, le Porte dur, pique-pique.*
14. **Boucher, Susan.** *big bella, tight piosh.*
15. **Brannen, Tim.** *balbott.*
16. **Breton, Rita.** *becuss, la Mittenne.*
17. **Campagna, Dan.** *bibbits, close the lights, coquottes, mous, where are you going, you?*

18. **Chabot, Wester Cecile.** *an-téka, en tout cas, bra-attelage, chtout fourré, je suis tout, chtedi, je te dis, chudanlune, je suis dans la lune, dretta lâ, droit la, kossé?, qu'est ce que c'est?, regarde la donc, Qu'est ce que tu fais la? ôte toé de d'la, Ote toi de la, Pi?, Et puis? Quesse tuveux ksam fasse, Qu'est ce que tu veux que ca me fasse? Ta tu d'javusah?, As tu jamais vu ca? Tu me crétu?, Me crois-tu? Vatendon, Vas t'en donc.*

19. **Chartrand, Janie.** *bankin, bulkhead, touk, wicked.*

20. **Connelly, Louise.** *ca pique, c'est bon, la bizoot, sodee, whip.*

21. **Conway, Roberta.** *Bernie & Dave's, Community Club, East Side, Mary's, Norwegian Village, The Green Front, The Irish Acre, The Narrows.*

22. **Cote, Eric.** *Elephant Mountain.*

23. **Croteau, Jess and Keith Blanchette.** *13 Mile Woods, Alcohol Springs, babout, beat the bonhomme, bibbit, Blanchettes Sausage, bob house, bonhomme, Bud Man, Bulldog sauce, Chinese pie, crut de nee, Dead River, DP, eeeh ma tante, Fyshy Coctail, Grill Candy, Le Grand Bois du Nord, Monaco to Jericho, moussie, pishou, piton, poutine, scatain, snowmachine, Swamp Donkeys, tabar noush.*

24. **Danais, Romeo.** *petauer.*

25. **Danderson, Clark.** *Berlin Brown Trout, deadhead, logdrive.*

26. **Dodge, Lisa.** *hice, keep the kids, cut true my yard, put out the lights.*

27. **Dube, Sister Theresa.** *on va a la fall.*

28. **Dumont, Michael.** *bi-bit, ginnig, mousse.*

29. **Ducan, Jim.** *muckaluck.*

30. **Dyer, Bill.** *Vinkerville.*

31. **Founier, Donald N.** *obedon or au bedon, oyons.*

32. **Gendron, Dr. Barry.** *fesses.*

33. **Ivory, Jeanne.** *13-mile woods, barbotte, batouille, Berlin Mills, Brown Company Store, Cascade Hill, crepes, Mary's, Mona's Restaurant, Norwegian Village, Pool Room, ration books, salvage, Sinibaldi's, The Arena, The Jungle, The Club, The Flats, The Jump, twinkies.*

34. **Jackson, Shirley.** *river rats.*

35. **L'Heureux, Rebecca.** *tatones, 'tit guy.*

36. **Lachance, Louise.** *pitonne.*

37. **LaPierre, Carla.** *minew, mumune.*

38. **Lavoie, Lucille.** *boudin, Chinese pie.*

39. **Lefebvre, Tracy.** *Chinese pie, DB, kushi, poutine.*

40. **Mackin, Dan.** *graveyard.*

41. **Marquis, Shawn.** *chicka-blaow, Eeee, franglais, Horne's Field Stonehenge, minu, piton, roost, sliding, the dirt road, the East Side Mall, the Sari-Sari Shop, the Tombola, the water tower, scroggin', the Rainbow Shop, WBRL.*

42. **Martel, Chris.** *Flock Mill, four by twice, grutone.*

43. **Montminy, Jasmine.** *chein qui passé, étou, meme, muss, ninune, pitoune, wiggamagig.*

44. **Montminy, Rachel.** *au bain, Cannuk, chochonerie, cocue, guinigue, mononce, okiedoke, oubedon, riggin, torchon.*

45. **Morgan Perry, Theresa.** *a guog dons, en falle, sodee.*

46. **Morin Migetz, Roberta.** *ca flippe? capo, swetteur.*

47. **Morin Pasciak, Lorraine.** *cremonne.*

48. **Morin St. Pierre, Benita.** *butiin.*

49. **Morrisette, Sister Cecile and the Sisters of the Presentation of Mary.** *arguine, arrête de baver, arrête de limoner, arrête de shinger, arrêtte de babiner, baroutette, bécosee, braquette (broquette), c'est baveu, ca fait dur, galendor, grouillle-toé, il mouille, l'eau blanche, l'esprit du clocher, le temps se chagrine, lève ta savate, mange du navo (navet), met ça sur la corniche, met de 'leau dans la bombe, met la soupe sure le poïle, moé , mon chou, noire come le poîle , noisette, toé, va à la potiquerre, va acheter de la carasine, va te choucher.*

50. **Nadeau, Jackie.** *Berlin Heights, Berlin Heights Addition, East Side, Forbush Park, Irish Acres, Jericho, Liberty Park, Napert Village, Norwegian Village, Petit Canada, Ramsey Hill, St. Gilles, The Avenues.*

51. **Oleson, Rev Gerald.** *Eee crow, piton, tahbanoosh.*

52. **Paquet, Linda.** *dinner and supper, dungarees, sour de sire.*

53. **Payeur, Melanie.** *do dos, porta potat,*

54. **Poulin, Dick.** *on va a fallé.*

55. **Poulin, Linda.** *eh maudis, eh torrieu, chaussure, pantoufle.*

56. **Ramsey, Dave.** *matante, monuncle, Pare a cinquante, Slaq a quarante.*

57. **Richards, Kris.** *Eeee *%@#$*

58. **Roberge, Jennie.** *Crystal Falls, touk.*

59. **Robege, Larry.** *Bernie and Dave's, con fil, pissenlit, Le Rendezvous du Roi.*

60. **Roberge, Susan.** *the seven, petes de la soeur.*

61. **Robichaud, Peter.** *Chinese pie, cookie, eee *@!$.*

62. **Ross, Kelly.** *Trow me down da stairs my sweater me, da Rich, tree, tings.*

63. **Roy, Ben.** *banking, eeee.*

64. **Roy, Darlene.** *Sideways, tunaburger.*

65. **Sanchargrin, Guy.** *bibit, brenleu, can-a-rabish, char, Pate chinois, tete-de-pioche.*

66. **Stanley, George.** *absolutely, pupcorn.*

67. **Sullivan Nicotra, Celia.** *quette.*

68. **Szumierz, Jan.** *pitounne, pitou, pass the mop.*

69. **Thompson, Lisa.** *scunion.*

70. **Vaillancourt, Angela and Becky Roberge.** *bino, do the groceries, gaz, good 'n you?, minew, pichou, quette, she got her baby, side by each, The Rich, Walmarts.*

71. **Vasquez, Carolyn.** *fesses, minous.*

72. **Villeneuve Rennison, Claire.** *cel, culotte, lampe, lassiette, ongle, pouèvre, tourcaire.*

73. **Welch, Amy.** *mouss.*

74. **Name Withheld.** *go downstreet, have a tree, I was to Concord yesterday.*

---

75. **Robert Perreault.** *Special edits and commentary including etymology.*

References and Berlin Resources

City of Berlin
http://www.berlinnh.gov/

Historical Society
http://www.historicalsocietynh.org/

LogJam
http://www.myspace.com/boompier/

Moffet House
http://www.aannh.org/heritage/coos/moffett.php

Nansen Ski Jump
http://www.skinansen.com/history.html/

Participate in the Project

If you have a word you would like to submit please send it along to berlindictionary@gmail.com.

Please include the following:

Word

Part of Speech

Definition

Translation if needed

Example Sentence

Once you have submitted the words you will be asked to sign a release form to allow them to be included in the next book or website. If enough words are collected, a second edition may be printed.

About the Author

 Rachelle Beaudoin was born and raised in Berlin NH on the West Side near the Ramsey Hill neighborhood.
She attended Holy Cross and the Rhode Island School of Design. Her artwork involves video, performance and now participatory books. Besides making art she enjoys playing hockey, weightlifting and spending time with her husband Steven Roberge and their dog Theo.

This book was typeset in Palatino.

The illustrations were drawn with pencil and marker.